Five Lies of Our Anti-Christian Age
Study Guide

Five Lies of Our
Anti-Christian Age
Study Guide

Rosaria Butterfield

WHEATON, ILLINOIS

SHGR			32	31	30	29	28	27	26	25	24	23
15	14	13	12	11	10	9	8	7	6	5	4	3	2	1

Contents

How This Study Works

*We are of no good to God or our loved ones if we believe the lies
the culture feeds us about what it means to be a man or a woman.*

AS YOU ENGAGE WITH CULTURE on multiple levels—in the news and on social media
and around your dinner table—you can tell that lies about gender are being told and
believed, and you want to uncover the truth. You want to explore the story culture is
telling about gender and expose the lies. And you want to be an agent of truth-telling
and positive influence so that you are useful to God and your loved ones. That's why
you're reading *Five Lies of Our Anti-Christian Age* and why you've decided to dig deeper
by going through the questions in this study guide.

The topics this book discusses are hot-button issues, and culture has a lot to say about
them. Given that reality, Rosaria's book contains some ideas and assertions to which you
will probably want to shout, "Yes! Amen!" It also contains some ideas and assertions that
may surprise you or make you want to argue with the author. You may even be tempted to
throw it across the room at some points. That's okay. Commit to the struggle, for it is in the
wrestling that we get stronger and in the digging that we reveal the beautiful gem of truth.
Here are two important ways to position yourself for growth as you interact with new ideas:

1. *Come with the right heart.* Before you get started, humbly ask the Lord to reveal
    himself and his truth to you. Commit yourself to obeying the truth he reveals
    through the Scriptures quoted and the wisdom presented. And then get ready
    to be challenged, inspired, and at points maybe even shocked.

2. *Persevere to the end.* Keep wrestling with the ideas—even the ones you disagree with—until you've thought them all the way to their logical conclusion. If you've been steeped in the lies of culture, it may take a while to see the truth. Be patient with the process and don't give up.

How This Study Works

This book is a study guide, which means it is designed to help you think and interact with the content of the book *Five Lies of Our Anti-Christian Age* and relevant Scripture passages. Some chapters have only a few questions; others have more. The point is to reach deeper understanding and insight, so don't be surprised or discouraged if some chapters take you more than one sitting to get through.

While this guide is designed for individual use to delve deeply into the content of *Five Lies of Our Anti-Christian Age*, it is also perfect for use in a group setting. If you're using this study guide in a small group or book study, you may want to select key questions to discuss and leave the others for members to consider on their own.

Introduction

We All Live in Babel Now

"The world is in chaos, and the church is divided because we have failed to obey God and value his plan for how men and women should live. We foolishly believed that we could permanently extricate the gospel from the creation ordinance—that we could have the New Testament without the Old. We foolishly believed that personal piety and love for Jesus required no doctrinal integrity and no foundation in the Bible as God's inerrant, sufficient, and inspired word. We foolishly believed that we could reinvent our calling as men and women, defy God's pattern and purpose for the sexes, and somehow reap God's blessing" (p. 6).

1. What are some words you've seen redefined and confused in popular culture?

2. What are some examples of how the church is failing to follow God's plan for men and women, and what divisions and debates has this led to?

_____

_____

The Creation of Man and Woman

3. Read Genesis 1:27–28. What do these verses tell us about men and women?

_____

_____

_____

_____

4. What do you think is the functional difference between being made *in* God's image and being made *as* God's image?

_____

_____

_____

_____

5. We are made in the image of God as distinctly men or women, and we are called to reflect that image in knowledge, righteousness, and holiness as men and as women. What are some of the ways you are striving to reflect God's image specific to your gender?

_____

_____

_____

_____

_____

6. Why do we all "live in Babel" now?

7. Read Romans 1:21–28. What three exchanges are described in this passage?

8. The three exchanges found in Romans 1:21–26 have created the world we now inhabit. How does each one of these logically flow one from another?

The Five Lies

Rosaria outlines five lies that stem from these exchanges. Under each one, write whether you agree or disagree with the statement and why. When you're done reading the book, you can come back to this page and see how your understanding has changed.

9. Homosexuality is normal.

_____

_____

_____

_____

10. Being a spiritual person is kinder than being a biblical Christian.

_____

_____

_____

_____

11. Feminism is good for the world and the church.

_____

_____

_____

_____

12. Transgenderism is normal.

_____

_____

_____

_____

13. Modesty is an outdated burden that serves male dominance and holds women back.

_____

_____

_____

_____

Lies and Repentance

"Sins spin webs of confusion. Repentance breaks those webs and replaces sin with clarity" (p. 20).

14. Following the examples Rosaria gives from her own life, what lies have you believed specific to issues of gender confusion and homosexuality? Have you repented of these sins?

_____

_____

_____

_____

The Necessity of Godly Confrontation

"A confrontation is an act of respect. To confront a deeply held belief involves recognizing the different points of view at play. It means knowing that there is a difference between acceptance and approval. . . . It requires us to take the side of the Bible's witness and to embrace Christ's point of view over and against anything and anyone that offers a different gospel" (p. 22).

15. Why is respect a necessary precursor to confrontation? What happens if you confront without respect?

_____

_____

16. Have you personally confronted any of the five lies discussed in the book? If so, what were the circumstances that led you to do so, and what was the outcome?

17. What might be the consequences of leaving these lies unconfronted?

18. Why is it more loving to confront a lie than to try to coexist with it?

19. What are the characteristics of godly confrontation?

20. In what ways does the church become less safe for people who experience homosexual desires when it embraces LBGTQ+ worldviews and vocabulary?

21. The world says if your daughter wants to become your son, you must comply or she will kill herself. Her therapist asks, "Would you rather have a dead daughter or a living son?" What is the gospel response to this (unfair) question?

22. Are people who live apart from God's creation ordinance victims in need of civil rights or sinners in need of a Savior? Do we love our neighbor enough to tell the truth?

23. In your own life, how have you experienced freedom after the application of biblical truth to areas of spiritual blindness and sin?

_____

_____

_____

_____

LIE #1

———————

HOMOSEXUALITY
IS NORMAL

CHAPTER 1

Once Gay, Always Gay?

1. Rosaria describes singing Psalm 113 as starting on safe ground and ending in the patriarchy she believed was "abusive male domination and institutional misogyny" (p. 40). Have you ever had a similar experience where a passage from the Bible started on safe ground and ended up hitting you between the eyes? Describe that experience.

_____

_____

_____

_____

_____

2. Read Psalm 113, then Genesis 1:26; 3:16. How do these verses add context to Psalm 113?

_____

_____

_____

_____

_____

3. How might you answer a friend who is offended by the idea that a woman can find her reward at home?

_____

_____

_____

_____

4. Explain this statement in your own words: "God's law is presented as a logical and obvious interpretation of what total depravity reveals about my heart" (p. 44). How does this statement inform your understanding of Psalm 113?

_____

_____

_____

_____

5. The author wondered which story was true, the biblical one or the feminist one. What are some helpful ways to come alongside someone who is sorting through life-shaking questions like these?

_____

_____

_____

_____

6. What practices or habits have helped you when you are grappling with ways in which your life doesn't line up with biblical truth?

_____

_____

_____

_____

_____

"My life as a lesbian seemed to invite me to participate in something deeper and larger than my small world and good for the future of the world. It gave me a team jersey and a position on the field" (p. 45).

7. How does that statement support or conflict with how you think lesbians view their sexual choices?

_____

_____

_____

_____

_____

8. How can Christians lovingly invite someone who chooses a homosexual lifestyle for these reasons into the life of faith?

_____

_____

_____

_____

_____

"Lesbianism in light of Scripture is a rejection of men in general and the creation ordinance in particular. Lesbianism rejects the creation cosmology—the nature of the universe. Calling lesbianism good and holy meant denying that God planted the seeds of the gospel in the garden" (p. 46).

9. How does lesbianism reject men, the creation ordinance, and in turn the gospel?

_____

_____

_____

_____

10. Why does this necessarily mean that a person can't have a lesbian identity with Christ?

_____

_____

_____

_____

"My feminist worldview valued boldness and strength and regarded gentleness and kindness as weaker virtues, reserved only for safe spaces, and dangerous in any patriarchal hierarchy" (p. 46).

11. Read Galatians 5:22–23. How are boldness and strength, gentleness and kindness all part of the Christian walk? In what contexts have you seen them coexist in the life of a believer?

_____

_____

12. Which aspects of the fruit of the Spirit come most naturally to you?

13. How have you sought to grow in the areas that are more challenging to you?

14. Godly womanhood does not erase a woman's strength or identity; rather, it applies God's grace to her. Describe women you know who are strong and embrace godly womanhood.

15. What do you think is the secret to embracing attributes that sometimes seem to be at odds with one another?

_____

_____

_____

"After my conversion, I noticed my affections changing. It wasn't instantaneous—like a combustion—but union with Christ was something that I could perceive growing inside me. . . . No one told me to pray the gay away. Because every sermon told me to drive a fresh nail into every sin every day, no one needed to" (p. 48).

16. What is your initial response to Rosaria's testimony of coming to understand her lesbianism as "a willful transgressive action"? Skepticism? Anger? A hearty "amen"? Write your honest thoughts below. You'll probably want to refer back to this when you finish the book.

_____

_____

_____

17. Read Colossians 3:9–10. What are some practices that you have put off, things that belong to your old self—and how have you sought to do that? What are some practices that you are striving to put on, things that are renewed in the image of your Creator?

_____

_____

"Taking care of my children provides a weight, a way to balance and measure the other good things to which God calls me. My husband provides a covering and a boundary. . . . My life has balance and momentum, borders and a shield. Far from holding me back, my role as a submitted wife to a godly husband has given me liberty and purpose" (p. 53).

18. Practically speaking, how might a single woman with no children participate in the model of godly womanhood as presented in Psalm 113? How have you seen this lived out?

19. Rosaria describes standing at the crossing of three divergent paths, each mutually exclusive: returning to her career at Syracuse University, taking on a role in administrative leadership, or becoming a homemaker. What advice would you have given her if she had asked you at that point, and why?

20. What similar decision points have you faced, and how did you choose between good options? Did your understanding of biblical patriarchy have any influence on your deliberations or final decision? If so, how?

_____

_____

_____

_____

"I don't embrace biblical patriarchy because I think men are good. . . . I embrace biblical patriarchy because men are *not* good (Jer. 17:9). Because men are not good, I am grateful to have godly men around who can defend and protect me against the roaming ravages of evil men who truly are wolves" (p. 54).

21. How does biblical patriarchy protect against the sin of men?

_____

_____

_____

_____

22. How can biblical patriarchy rightly understood and applied help a woman who is in an abusive situation?

_____

_____

_____

_____

_____

"Sanctification is a gift of God's grace, but only when we participate in our own sanctification are we renewed in the image of God. Our obedience, then, reflects the integrity and authenticity of our faith. Our obedience is a duty and a joy. If this is not the case, we have reason to worry about the state of our soul" (pp. 54–55).

23. Sanctification involves a change in our affections and our actions. What part does God play in this process?

_____

_____

_____

_____

_____

24. What is our role in sanctification?

_____

_____

_____

_____

_____

CHAPTER 2

What Is Intersectionality?

"Intersectionality creates a grand story, a metanarrative, out of oppression. It maintains that the world is made up of power struggles, and that white, male, heterosexual patriarchy must be destroyed to liberate those who are oppressed by it. It understands the biblical complementarity of husbands and wives as perverted and 'weaponized.'" It believes that if we can expose the myriad ways in which people suffer down to the smallest detail and then rearrange the power oppressions, we can change the storyline of a person's history (of oppression) and destiny (of liberation)" (p. 59).

1. Using the definition of intersectionality above, what areas have you seen this play out in culture in addition to sexual orientation?

_____

_____

_____

_____

_____

Keep these specific categories in mind as you answer the rest of the questions so you can provide concrete examples as you think through the implications of intersectionality.

2. Choose one of the categories you thought of for the question above and identify:

- the oppressor
- the oppression
- the victim
- the liberation narrative

_____

_____

_____

_____

_____

3. What additional insights does naming these categories reveal about the lies that are being told and believed?

_____

_____

_____

_____

_____

4. The most believable lies have some truth in them, only it's twisted. What are the grains of truth in intersectionality?

_____

_____

_____

_____

5. What Christian virtues does intersectionality appeal to or mimic?

6. How do intersectionality's attempts at mercy and justice contrast with biblical definitions of these virtues?

"Intersectionality fails to distinguish between morally neutral categories of lived experience (race and ethnicity) with morally charged ones (homosexuality and transgenderism). Because intersectionality lacks a biblical category of sin, it instead multiplies sins of its own making" (p. 61).

7. Intersectionality works at cross-purposes with the Bible. In what ways is its view of human identity at odds with the biblical understanding of identity?

8. What practical difference does it make to define identity in gospel terms rather than the terms of intersectionality?

_____

_____

_____

_____

9. How does intersectionality view or define sin? In what ways is this out of line with the Bible's view of sin?

_____

_____

_____

_____

10. How does intersectionality affect a person's view of repentance and grace?

_____

_____

_____

11. In what ways does intersectionality produce social fragmentation and human division?

_____

_____

12. How does intersectionality lead to punishing the good and celebrating evil?

13. What answer does the gospel offer for intersectionality?

"The church's embrace of intersectionality as an analytical tool was intended to give voice to the voiceless. But the victimized identities that emerge from intersectionality are perpetually immature and in constant need of therapy and affirmation" (p. 62).

14. How have you seen intersectionality enter the church?

15. What were the unintended consequences in the church of embracing this lie?

_____

_____

_____

_____

CHAPTER 3

What Are Homosexual Orientation and Gay Christianity?

"Homosexual orientation is a man-made theory about anthropology, or what it means to be human. It comes from atheistic worldviews that coalesced in the nineteenth century in Europe. Homosexual orientation is not a biblical concept, nor can it be manipulated in the service of Christian living" (p. 65).

1. What sources have informed your view of homosexuality up to this point?

_____

_____

_____

_____

"Sigmund Freud and Charles Darwin . . . both contributed to the general idea of sexual orientation, the idea that human beings are oriented—aimed, directed, pitched—by sexual desires, understood as an internal, organic drive over which we have no control" (pp. 65–66).

2. What are the practical consequences of defining sexual orientation in these terms?

_____

_____

3. The biblical mandate places sexuality "under God's divine order for his created purposes" (p. 66). What are the practical consequences of defining sexuality in biblical terms? In other words, how would a person who embraces the biblical understanding of sexuality live?

_____

_____

_____

_____

4. Read Leviticus 18:22; 20:13; Romans 1:26–27; 1 Corinthians 6:9–11; and 1 Timothy 1:9–10. How do these passages define homosexuality? Are there any things about these passages that surprise you?

_____

_____

_____

_____

"The Romantic period is typified by an uncontested embrace of personal experience, not merely as self-expression or self-representation, but also as the way in which we know truth (epistemology). For the first time in the history of the world, personal feelings were now believed to be the fount of truth. Romanticism introduced the idea of 'my personal truth'—and with this concept, we lost all standards by which to measure objective truth" (pp. 69–70).

5. How did the historical context of Romanticism pave the way for the church to embrace homosexuality?

_____

_____

_____

_____

6. Interact with the assertion that "the witness of the evangelical church on the subject of homosexuality expresses more corporate sin than saving grace" (p. 67). Do you agree or disagree? Support your answer.

_____

_____

_____

_____

7. What theological safeguards—and specific Bible passages—should have protected the church from the lie that homosexuality is normal?

_____

_____

_____

_____

8. In what ways does separating homosexual identity from practice and declaring it blessed by the Bible reject the doctrines of

- creation
- sin
- repentance
- sanctification

9. In what ways does separating homosexual identity from practice reject the Bible as inerrant, infallible, sufficient, and authoritative?

"The nineteenth-century category of sexual orientation reflects Romanticism's claims on truth, redefining men and women from people who are made in God's image with souls that will last forever to people whose sexual perversion and gender confusion define, liberate, and dignify them. . . . The nineteenth century ushered in a new measure of man—one in which sexual desires, self-conceptions, and practices are defining of personhood. In this climate, the idea of a homosexual orientation was born, and it served to create a fictional identity that robbed people of their true one: being made in the image of God with creational purposes" (pp. 70–71).

10. Looking at the news just in the last week, what examples can you find of popular culture situating sexuality in personal identity?

11. Where have you seen this happen in the church?

12. How would you respond to the assertion that heterosexuality is as fallen as homosexuality? In what ways are heterosexual sins disordered? What sets them apart as different in terms of the male/female pattern of creation?

Gay Christianity

"Like the secular LGBTQ+ movement, the gay Christian one operates under the notion that homosexuality is 'normal' and that calling it a normal variance is kindness. Gay Christianity believes that sexual orientation accurately organizes humanity into fixed, morally neutral expressions of sexual desire. Side A is 'gay-affirming,' meaning that it invents biblical support for gay marriage and full inclusion of people who identify as

LGBTQ+ in the leadership and membership of the church. Side B is 'nonaffirming' of gay sex. Additionally, it elevates celibacy and singleness as God's highest calling while heartily embracing homosexual orientation" (p. 73 and 73n8).

13. Are you familiar with these two distinctions of gay Christianity, and where have you encountered them?

_____

_____

_____

_____

14. Have you supported one or the other of these viewpoints?

_____

_____

_____

_____

"Both Sides A and B believe that homosexuality is fixed and that the gospel might change people in smaller ways but never in the deep matters of sexual desire. . . . The gospel, according to gay Christianity, features a Jesus who loves you just as you are. He asks you to repent of sins of injustice, materialism, and lack of love, but he has nothing to say about your homosexuality. . . . The most intimate connection for the gay Christian is born through shared same-sex attraction" (pp. 74–75).

15. From what you read in this chapter, summarize where this idea of gay Christianity originated and identify the lies in these beliefs.

_____

_____

16. Much of both Side A and Side B gay Christianity involve replacing biblical terms like *sin*, *temptation*, and *healing* with words like *sublimation*, *aesthetic orientation*, and *sexual minority*. What theological words have you seen replaced with cheap counterfeits or half-truths in Christian circles?

17. What effect does it have on congregations and Christian educational institutions if a pastor or leader uses these culturally fashionable terms rather than biblical language?

18. Christians with homosexual desires often try to navigate their sexual orientation rather than repent from the sin of homosexual desires or practice, seek forgiveness through the blood of Christ, pursue greater sanctification, and seek freedom from these sins. How are these attempts a redefinition of the biblical concept of sanctification?

19. Read Matthew 5:21–28. How do Jesus's words inform your understanding of

- desire
- sin
- repentance

20. Is a Christian struggling with homosexual desire a victim who suffers and should be pitied, or a sinner who needs repentance and growth in sanctification? Defend your answer using biblical terms and truths.

21. Where are Christians who view themselves as victims or sexual minorities ultimately putting their hope?

"Temptation is to be fought through grace. But that does not mean that sinful temptations should ever be whitewashed or miscategorized. Sin is our enemy, not our friend" (p. 81).

22. Read 2 Corinthians 5:17 and Ephesians 4:22–24. How might this discussion of homosexual temptation change the way you fight other temptations you face?

23. Rosaria offers a three-pronged alternative to the Revoice movement: (1) worship God in a true branch of a Bible-believing church; (2) apply the means of grace to your daily life; (3) deal with sin in God's way—repent and walk in the light. How might each of these three things aid someone struggling with homosexual desire?

CHAPTER 4

Why Is Homosexuality a Sin When It Feels Normal to Some People?

1. Chapter 4 is titled, "Why Is Homosexuality a Sin When It Feels Normal to Some People?" What was your first reaction to the question posed by the chapter title?

_____

_____

_____

_____

_____

2. Read Colossians 3:1–5. What does this passage say about the effect the gospel should have on behavior and desire in the life of a believer?

_____

_____

_____

_____

_____

3. Read Mark 7:20–23 and Ephesians 4:22–24.

  • What do these verses say about the source of sin?
  • What do they say about the battle against sinful desire?

_____

_____

_____

_____

4. Read Romans 6:3–11. What hope do we have if sinful desire lurks so deeply in the human heart?

_____

_____

_____

_____

5. Practically speaking, what does it look like for you to live united with Christ? What habits and practices are involved?

_____

_____

_____

_____

6. What does it mean to put sin to death? What habits and practices are involved in this battle?

"Union with Christ is this dynamic and supernatural power that God gives his redeemed people, but you cannot have union with Christ if you have made an identity out of anything else. Union with Christ demands that Christ has exclusive claims on his redeemed people" (p. 93).

7. Why is trying to maintain a homosexual identity incompatible with Christian faith?

What If It Feels Right?

"We manifest our faith by believing that the Bible is truer than our feelings. This is what authentic faith in Jesus Christ looks like" (p. 95).

8. What is an example of something you believe based on the Bible that goes against your feelings?

Indoctrination, Empathy, and the New Religion of Homosexuality

"In a pagan paradigm, the problem is that we have failed to achieve unity with other people, and the solution is that we need to look within ourselves to find the power and love to change" (p. 97).

9. In what ways has homosexuality become a false religion? Think of the aspects that are part of most religions and define what fulfills those roles in the homosexual movement.

_____

_____

_____

_____

"In a biblical paradigm, the problem is that we have rejected God's authority by refusing to obey the Bible as it is written. We disobey his laws, and we don't like his solutions. What is his solution? The solution is to look to God for repentance and accept the sacrifice of Jesus for us" (p. 97).

10. How can Christians properly engage those who claim to be both gay and Christian to help them see the reality that they are rejecting the Bible and hurting themselves and others?

_____

_____

_____

"The only way out of the ever-damning homosexual repetition, the constant hunger for the elusive depth of knowing and being known, is repentance for sin, even repentance for a sin that feels natural. And after repentance must come renewal—which requires a complete break with all sinful patterns and the people and entertainment venues in which these patterns lurk. It all comes down to this: Do you trust your feelings, or do you trust the word of God? Do you perceive your feelings through the word of God, or do you perceive the word of God through your feelings? Do your feelings know you best, or does the God who made you?" (pp. 98–99).

11. Thinking of your own life, in what areas do you struggle to trust the word of God over your feelings?

Do We Need Empathy or Sympathy?

12. How would you describe the difference between empathy and sympathy?

13. What are some situations in which empathy is warranted, and what does that look like?

14. Is empathy ever a bad thing? Explain.

_____

_____

_____

_____

15. Sympathy recognizes a problem that someone else has, and sympathy grieves and longs for a solution. Why does the distinction between empathy and sympathy matter when we are talking about how we should respond to people who embrace homosexuality?

_____

_____

_____

_____

"If the highest form of love is standing in someone else's shoes, no one is left standing in a place of objective truth. If someone is drowning in a river, jumping in with him may break up his loneliness, but having two drowned people produces an even greater problem. Sympathy allows someone to stand on the shore, on the solid ground of objective truth where real help might be found" (p. 101).

16. How can we show sympathy to someone who is caught in homosexual desire?

_____

_____

17. Read Hebrews 4:14–16. How can these verses help us in our own struggle against sin and as we strive to help others?

_____

_____

_____

_____

The Need to Know Jesus

"Jesus suffers with us, but Jesus does not sin with us. He will cure us on his terms, which include stepping into the power that his resurrection offers to fight sin every day of our life on earth. His power to resist temptation is given to us by grace" (p. 103).

18. Read John 5:1–15. How can this story inform your approach to people struggling with homosexual desire?

_____

_____

_____

_____

_____

Come to the Throne of Grace

"How sad indeed for someone who is already weighed down by sin to be denied the true remedy for the problem. That is what gay Christianity does. It denies the sexual sinner repentance and immerses her in the futile task of trying to domesticate her sin. Trying to deal with sin in your own flesh is what Pharisees always encourage" (p. 108).

19. How has your understanding of homosexual desire changed as you have engaged with these chapters?

_____

_____

_____

_____

_____

20. How are you being convicted to change in the way you relate to the church as it wrestles with the issue of homosexuality and friends or loved ones who embrace a homosexual identity? Make these matters for prayer and repentance.

_____

_____

_____

_____

———————

BEING A SPIRITUAL PERSON IS KINDER THAN BEING A BIBLICAL CHRISTIAN

CHAPTER 5

Where Is God—in an Ancient Book or in Me?

1. Reading the story of Jessica, what kind of help or advice might you have offered if you had known the issues she was struggling with?

_____

_____

_____

_____

2. What parts of her story ring true to your experience, either personally or with a loved one? What have you learned from those faith struggles?

_____

_____

_____

_____

3. What parts of Jeremy's worldview have you encountered personally? How did you respond to those arguments?

_____

_____

_____

_____

_____

"While you can't be saved by your theology, you can be taken dangerously off course by an unbiblical one" (p. 121).

4. Digging deeper into Jeremy's reaction, what were some of the theological lies he was believing? Where have you encountered those lies in your life?

_____

_____

_____

_____

_____

5. What were some of the theological lies Jessica was believing, and how did those make her vulnerable to Jeremy's influence?

_____

_____

_____

_____

_____

6. What truths do you think Jessica needed to hear?

_____

_____

_____

_____

It's Still All Very Personal

"My conversion hinged not on what my flesh craved but on who Jesus is. Who Jesus is and what the Bible is are inseparable. Jesus is alive, and so is the Bible. And that is what set it apart from all the other books on my shelf that denied him" (p. 122).

7. In your own life, identify some areas in which you have tried to separate who Jesus is from what the Bible says. What parts of the Bible have you struggled to believe and obey?

_____

_____

_____

_____

8. What has helped you gain victory over those areas of faith struggle?

_____

_____

_____

_____

What Is the Difference between Unbiblical Spirituality and Biblical Faith?

"In *The Other Worldview: Exposing Christianity's Greatest Threat*, author Peter Jones says that it is not only the lack of genuinely converted Christians in the church but also the destruction of Christian culture that has made our world unsafe, unsavory, and unrecognizable: 'Many of the traditional plausibility structures that gave life meaning and significance under Christian influence in the West are unrecognizable:

- Morality is relativized by varied (and often contradictory) personal or social conventions.
- Honesty means being true to one's inner commitments and longing more than to external expectations or objective facts.
- Acceptable models of sexuality and family allow various combinations of persons and genders.
- Marriage is often functionally indistinguishable from mutually convenient cohabitation.
- Motherhood is celebrated in the same breath with abortion on demand' "[1] (p. 123).

9. How have you seen these false beliefs infiltrate the church?

_____

_____

_____

_____

10. How have you seen the church successfully counter these influences and beliefs?

_____

_____

_____

_____

---

1 Peter Jones, *The Other Worldview: Exposing Christianity's Greatest Threat* (Bellingham, WA: Kirkdale Press, 2015), 4.

What Happens When People Dress Their Christian Faith in Pagan Clothes?

11. What instances have you seen of the church embracing culture in an attempt to be missional?

_____

_____

_____

_____

12. What is wrongheaded about this approach? Why can cultural spirituality not coexist with biblical Christianity? What doctrines must be dismissed and what vices must be celebrated in order to embrace cultural spirituality?

_____

_____

_____

_____

13. What biblical virtues should Christians exhibit when they are confronting the lies of unbiblical spirituality?

_____

_____

_____

_____

14. Kent said, "When we love Jesus first, we love others safely. When we love others first, we don't love others safely." Explain why this is true.

....

....

....

....

"The gospel doesn't just make us nicer versions of ourselves. The gospel gives us a new nature and the power to live for the glory of God" (p. 124).

CHAPTER 6

The Bible Knows Me Better than I Know Myself

1. Looking back over Ken's lecture on pages 130–143, what surprises you about how he communicates the story of the Bible?

_____

_____

_____

_____

_____

2. What surprises you about Rosaria's initial questions and responses?

_____

_____

_____

_____

_____

3. List all the theological truths Ken packed into his brief lecture.

4. How does a lecture like Ken's, which traces the storyline of the Bible, answer the questions posed by cultural spirituality?

5. How does the message of the Bible answer people's deepest questions about:

   • Who they are
   • Why they exist
   • What hope they have

6. Read Psalm 19:7–14. What does this passage say that Scripture does for us and in us?

_____

_____

7. How have you experienced these benefits of Scripture?

_____

_____

_____

_____

8. How might you engage an unbeliever or someone who embraces the lies of unbiblical spirituality with these ideas about the Bible?

_____

_____

_____

_____

LIE #3

FEMINISM IS GOOD FOR THE WORLD AND THE CHURCH

CHAPTER 7

Do You Know Yourself and How Do You Know?

1. Would you call yourself a feminist? Why or why not?

_____

_____

_____

_____

2. In what areas do you think the church is too embracing of feminism?

_____

_____

_____

_____

3. In what areas do you think the church fails to value women for the unique gifts they bring?

_____

_____

_____

_____

4. Read Proverbs 29:25. How might viewing the way you treat a prodigal child through the lens of pleasing God rather than pleasing man affect the way you relate to him or her?

_____

_____

_____

_____

5. How do you think you should respond if your daughter comes home declaring that she is living with her lesbian girlfriend or is engaged to marry her lesbian partner?

_____

_____

_____

_____

"Sin should affect us so profoundly that the 'nuanced' way that the world covers it up ought to feel repulsive. . . . When our children are living in sin, at the first sight of it, we must be cut to the heart. We must deal with sin at its first occurrence, no matter how pragmatically our society domesticates that sin. And our own sin should bring us to our knees with a sense of shame and remorse that far outweighs the sin of others" (p. 152).

6. When it comes to dealing with young adult children, how can we balance the desire to deal rightly with their sin and the need to accept them where they are?

_____

_____

7. Thinking of your own sin, how can you do better at dealing with sin rather than letting it fester and grow?

_____

_____

_____

_____

8. Are there sins you have been tolerating or domesticating that you need to repent of? What action steps will you take in this regard?

_____

_____

_____

_____

The First and Second Sin . . .

9. In your own life, where have you seen evidence of the second sin being worse than the first?

_____

_____

_____

_____

"The worldview of feminism, like that of homosexual rights, has powerfully persuaded Christians that those certain areas designated 'women's rights' are off-limits to biblical scrutiny. The category sacred to feminism is women's equality with men in all things—to the point of denying the creation ordinance and basic biology. Under feminism, men and women are interchangeable. Under Scripture, such interchangeability is sin" (p. 154).

10. What is the functional difference between calling men and women "equally made in the image of God" and calling them "interchangeable"? How can one do the first without falling into the trap of the second?

11. What are some ways the church can embrace and affirm the equality of women without falling into the trap of feminism?

The Knowledge of God and That of Ourselves Are Connected

12. What evidence does Rosaria offer that "feminism is incompatible with biblical personhood because it contradicts the creation ordinance"? Do you agree or disagree, and why?

"We image bearers of a holy God are so hardened by sin that we don't see our rebellion. We call it *liberty, progress, feminism,* but God sees it as rejecting the brightness of glory, scorning our designated roles and places as kings and queens. We scoff at the glory God holds out for us when we deny the biblical gender roles he has reserved for his daughters" (p. 156).

13. Thinking specifically of the ways the church embraces feminism, how do these ways reject the glory God offers for women?

"Man and woman together are jewels of the same crown. The roles that women are blessed to embody cannot be replaced by a man. And likewise the roles that men are blessed to embody cannot be replaced by a woman. This is not a matter of competence, creativity, or modern medicine. God himself is holding the order and pattern of creation as a mandate for fruitful and good living" (p. 157).

14. What examples have you seen of men and women embracing their roles in a way that celebrates the image of God in gender?

15. What examples have you seen of Christian men and women striving to erase the differences between their genders?

_____

_____

_____

"At its most basic distinction, God created men for strength, women for nurturance, and both for the other, her submission yielding to his headship creating the harmony of mutual work and worship of God. The simplicity, beauty, and perfection of the creation ordinance may be marred by sin but not by the designer's perfect plan" (p. 158).

16. Read Proverbs 31. What adjectives would you use to describe godly womanhood?

_____

_____

_____

_____

17. Do you think there is room in the biblical mandate for men to be the primary caregiver for the children? What circumstances would affect your answer?

_____

_____

_____

Submission Is Biblical, but Is It Dangerous?

"A Christian's best defense against abuse of all authority is membership in a biblically faithful church. Submission doesn't imply brainless passivity" (p. 162).

18. How will a wife know when she needs to go to the church to report an abuse issue?

_____

_____

_____

_____

19. What should she do if her church supports her husband in his abuse rather than supporting her?

_____

_____

_____

_____

CHAPTER 8

Does the Gospel Need a Feminist Rescue?

1. What experiences have shaped your views on gender roles (books, speakers, life events, interactions with Scripture)?

2. What experiences have shaped your views on abortion?

3. Read Genesis 2:7–25. What do these verses communicate about the purpose and pattern of marriage?

"Kevin DeYoung recounts five patterns that set us up for either grace or condemnation:

- Male leadership—(also known, from a biblical perspective, as patriarchy).
- Godly women arrayed with heroic characteristics.
- Godly women helping men.
- Ungodly women influencing men for evil, while ungodly men abuse women.
- Women finding meaning, grace, and suffering in bearing and caring for children.[2]

The power of these five patterns lies in not only what they communicate but also what they are. A pattern provides edges and direction. It tells us how to live and warns of the dangers of falling away. A pattern is to be followed, to be represented with accuracy, precision, and care. So we are to obey the Lord by copying his pattern in commands" (p. 170).

4. What edges or direction do these five patterns set for daily life in a marriage? What will obeying them look like in a marriage?

5. What edges or direction do they provide for daily life outside of marriage?

---

2   Kevin De Young, "Patterns That Preach," in *Men and Women in the Church: A Short, Biblical, Practical Introduction* (Wheaton, IL: Crossway, 2021), 36–42.

6. What areas of daily life do you think are left up to conscience; in other words, what decisions or habits fall outside of these five patterns?

_____

_____

_____

_____

"The creational order of biblical headship describes the biblical practice of responsible, caring, and sacrificial male leadership in the home and church. As a complement to the husband's leadership role, his wife, under her husband's leadership, helps steward God's creation and fulfill the creation mandate. Biblical headship is not an evil to be erased but rather God's design to run the wolves out of town. But Adam failed in his biblical headship; he failed to check the garden for the danger of an intruder, and he failed by obeying Eve's command to eat the forbidden fruit" (p. 171).

7. Read Genesis 3:4–6. What parts of the five patterns of biblical gender roles were disobeyed in the fall, and how?

_____

_____

_____

_____

8. How have you seen biblical headship principles help people steward God's creation and fulfill the creation mandate?

_____

_____

_____

_____

9. Read Ephesians 5:22–24, 31–33. What is the scriptural basis of a wife's submission?

10. What limits do these verses in Ephesians place on submission?

11. What should a submissive wife do when her husband fails?

"Being made by God's design according to the pattern of creation is therefore a statement about both what it means to be human and what it means to interpret a text with accuracy. Every person lives under the authority, influence, or manipulation of someone or something. Everyone lives under sovereignty, whether the sovereign is God or personal feelings or some evil tyrant" (p. 174).

12. Looking at the patterns and habits of your life, what is the biggest influence on your interpretation of gender roles?

_____

_____

13. What needs to change for you to order your life under the sovereignty of God rather than the sovereignty of feelings or other influences?

_____

_____

_____

_____

CHAPTER 9

The Power of a Woman's Voice

"Biblical patriarchy is a blessing, not a crime, and women who support biblical inerrancy and the fulfillment of biblical gender roles willingly and joyfully support and build up biblical patriarchy" (p. 177).

1. What is biblical patriarchy?

2. What is your view of biblical patriarchy, and what has shaped your view?

Jesus and John Wayne and Other Bad Ideas

"To a feminist, every problem comes down to patriarchy. This reveals an important distinction in how people interpret the Bible. Inerrantists—those who believe every word is inspired by God—read what the Bible says and interpret a text by allowing Scripture to interpret Scripture. Feminists read the Bible for what it might say or could say" (p. 180).

3. What theological issues do you tend to view through a feminist lens?

_____

_____

_____

_____

4. What effect does embracing a feminist interpretation of Scripture have on individual Christians?

_____

_____

_____

_____

5. What effect does embracing a feminist interpretation of Scripture have on the church?

_____

_____

_____

_____

"For almost all of church history, a Christian was defined as someone who upheld the truth of Scripture—both the truth of the meaning of the words themselves and the living power of the book itself. For almost all of church history, we did not quibble over the meaning of every word that crossed us. A word stood for its plain meaning as it would have been understood at the time the Bible was written. In today's modern evangelical culture, a Christian is a Christian if she says she is. This 'self-ID' approach to truth is both dangerous and foolish. The Christian faith is about lived obedience to the word of God, not verbal affirmation" (p. 181).

6. Where have you encountered the "self-ID" approach to truth? What were the practical implications of that approach?

"We need to ask the question, If the biblical account of creation cannot be trusted to teach us about what makes women distinct, where ought we to go for this insight? This is where the usefulness of feminism as a gospel frame crumbles in the foolishness that it is. It wants an essential and distinct women's voice at the same time that it rejects a biblical origin for what makes a woman distinct. Without a biblical basis for sexual difference, any feminist enterprise crumbles" (p. 188).

7. What does the Bible say about women's worth? Use Bible references to support your answer.

8. What does the Bible say about women's purpose or calling? Use Bible references to support your answer.

_____

_____

_____

_____

9. What does the feminist view say about the source of women's worth?

_____

_____

_____

_____

10. What does the feminist view declare a woman's purpose to be?

_____

_____

_____

_____

11. Why does a feminist view crumble when it loses its biblical roots?

_____

_____

_____

_____

12. Answer the questions we began with:

  • Why isn't feminism good for the world?
  • Why isn't feminism good for the church?

LIE #4

_____

TRANSGENDERISM
IS NORMAL

CHAPTER 10

The Sin of Envy

"Transgenderism will be the final nail in the coffin of feminism. Why? Because you cannot defend the civil rights of a woman if you don't know what she is. Transgenderism is the mark of a world that has swapped Christian morality for postmodern angst. A Christian needs to think about this. Is transgenderism something a person 'navigates' or repents of and heals from? Is transgenderism a sign of mental illness or sin?" (p. 193).

1. Have you known any transgendered people personally? How would you describe them?

2. What motivated their transgenderism?

3. Did they seem happy and at peace, or full of angst?

_____

_____

_____

_____

Pronouns, Battlefields, and Government Schools

"Because we have denigrated God's design by believing the lies of homosexuality, feminism, and transgenderism and have allowed false and true teaching to coexist by rejecting biblical inerrancy, the battlefield now rages dangerously for children" (p. 197).

4. Review Genesis 1:27–28. What parts of the creation mandate does transgenderism work against?

_____

_____

_____

_____

5. Have you encountered transgenderism in your local school? How did it manifest, and what were the consequences?

_____

_____

_____

_____

"There's a significant difference between an adult suffering from a mental or medical illness leading her into sinful envy, and a manipulated teenager or child under the influence of a social contagion that has snowballed into mass hysteria. Christians bear a responsibility to minister to both, as both are hurting people, but to help, we need to distinguish between the two and diagnose the problem accurately. The former, adults suffering from an illness, requires biblical counseling and Christian medical care. The latter, manipulated kids, requires that we protect them (and ourselves) from false teachers and remove them from government schools whenever possible" (pp. 199–200).

6. What are you personally doing—or what could you do—to help adults suffering from gender confusion?

_____

_____

_____

_____

7. What are you personally doing—or what could you do—to help children suffering from the influence of transgenderism in schools and in culture?

_____

_____

_____

_____

8. What is your church doing to help? Should your church be doing something different?

_____

_____

_____

_____

The Sin of Envy

"Envy is delusional entitlement masked in a package of victimhood and unbearable pain. If transgenderism is envy's modern face, then there is truly no such thing as a 'transgendered Christian,' if by this term we mean something celebrating a transgendered identity as somehow honoring to Christ or the church" (p. 202).

9. In your daily life, do you think of envy as a sin? What kinds of things do you tend to envy, and what, if anything, do you do to uproot this sin from your heart?

10. Read Proverbs 27:3–4 and 14:30, which describe the dangers of envy. What other sins does envy lead to?

11. What is the root of envy—what are its causes? How can naming the root causes help us to fight against envy in our hearts?

12. How is transgenderism a type of envy?

_____

_____

_____

_____

13. What other sins are evident in the transgendered movement?

_____

_____

_____

_____

"A physical diagnosis of gender dysphoria shows significant clinical distress arising from genetic, biological, environmental, or cultural factors. From a biblical perspective, gender dysphoria is a physical health problem, not only a mental health problem. And a Christian response to people with problems is to help. Godly help for the gender dysphoric is genuine love, godly compassion, biblical counseling, and potentially hormonal treatments that restore normal hormonal balance. Godly help for the gender dysphoric understands medical and psychiatric problems as serious and does not believe that a gay Pride parade, a _Blue's Clues_ sing-along, or an opportunity to appear in drag and read to children at a public library offers an adequate solution. Rather, these 'solutions' show a world given over to sin; a world where scandal barely rouses us from our stupor" (p. 203).

14. How can we disentangle the sin roots of transgenderism from the medical roots in a way that enables us to help people caught in its grip? If both physical illness and sexual sin come from the fall, how should Christians respond to the natural fallenness

of physical illness on the one hand, and the moral fallenness of homosexuality and transgenderism on the other?

_____

_____

_____

_____

"Even Spirit-wrought Christians must fight against the flesh. Reframing sinful deeds and desires of the flesh in worldly or therapeutic terms is sinful. It tells lies and betrays the power of God's election, Christ's redemption, and the Spirit's comfort. It rewrites the gospel, entangles the church into foolish debates, and confuses our young people. This is the appalling situation in which we find the evangelical church today. We who love the Lord have failed to love people deluded by sin in a biblical, godly, and courageous way. We who love the Lord have failed to drive the wolves out of our churches" (p. 204).

15. In what ways is the church enabling the sin of transgenderism to prosper?

_____

_____

_____

_____

16. Why is using people's preferred pronouns potentially harmful? What might be a loving and compassionate alternative?

_____

_____

_____

17. What might it look like to love a transgendered person who comes to your church in a gospel-affirming way?

18. What virtues do we need to pray for and exhibit when dealing with the issue of transgenderism in our communities?

19. How do the doctrines of grace, redemption, sanctification, and eternal life inform the way Christians should interact with:

- transgenderism as a concept?

• individuals we know who believe the lies of transgenderism?

_____

_____

_____

_____

_____

CHAPTER 11

The War of Words

"*Trans*" implies that original biological sex has no design pattern or purpose and therefore can be easily replaced by anything else if your feelings so dictate. And if your feelings are strong enough, this rewrites history and 'proves' that how you feel is who you have always been. It makes the false claim that who you are originally, deeply, really, is your psychological choice" (pp. 214–15).

1. Have you ever been accused of "misgendering" someone by failing to use (or remember) his or her "preferred" pronouns? What were the circumstances?

_____

_____

_____

_____

2. What is the logical fallacy in saying that how you feel is who you have always been?

_____

_____

_____

_____

3. In what other areas (besides gender) do Christians live as if feelings trump truth?

_____

_____

_____

_____

Understanding Today's Lingo

4. How would you explain the difference between gender dysphoria and transgenderism?

_____

_____

_____

_____

"The majority of children who experience gender anxiety will experience desistance through the normal process of growing up—85 percent by puberty and almost everyone else by adulthood. But hormone blockers will indeed block the normal way that the body will right itself. This is a very serious matter" (p. 216 and 216n4).

5. What personal experience (if any) do you have with transgender youth? How has your exposure to people who have this struggle or the things you have read in the media influenced your thinking and beliefs about transgenderism?

_____

_____

_____

_____

6. How do you think Christians should respond to a transgendered or gender dysphoric individual who walks into their church? What Scriptures or theological principles apply to this issue?

_____

_____

_____

_____

_____

7. How should Christian parents respond to their child who feels trapped in the wrong body or who has been indoctrinated by transgender ideology and wants to "transition"? What Scriptures or theological principles apply to this issue?

_____

_____

_____

_____

"We live in a culture that ascribes truth to feelings and perceptions, and it fears hurting people's feelings more than encouraging them to permanently mutilate their bodies. Christians must stand in a discerning place. Our culture says things like not being believed is more traumatic than abuse. But believing things that aren't true is a sin and leads people into further sin" (p. 217).

8. What are the dangers of attributing truth to feelings and perceptions?

_____

_____

9. How can we guard against this in the church?

"The tendency among teenage girls is to engage in *corumination*, the excessive sharing of hardships and negative feedback–seeking. Shrier summarizes:

> Teenage girls spread psychic illness because of features natural to their modes of friendship: co-rumination, excessive reassurance-seeking, and negative feedback-seeking, in which someone maintains a feeling of control by angling for confirmation of her low-concept from others. It isn't hard to see why the 24/7 forum of social media intensifies and increases the incidence of each.

> While my heart breaks for the girls who spend their time in the negative feedback loop of social media, corumination, and negative feedback–seeking, I can't help but wonder how Christian girls have ended up in this place" (pp. 220–21 and 220n11).

10. What do you think are some factors that have made today's teen and preteen girls susceptible to rapid-onset gender dysphoria?

11. What might be some solutions or tools to help us fight off these influences?

_____

_____

_____

_____

"Let's be clear: what is helpful here is sympathy and care, not political activism. To think that the pain of illness, disability, or moral corruption can be made better by a parade and a sticker and a slogan is vile, and Christians should hang their heads in shame if they endorse this. When a Christian responds to the natural effects of Adam's sin with faith, obedience, and good works, this brings glory to God and peace with God to the believer. When anyone responds to the natural effects of Adam's sin with envy and self-harm, this elicits God's anger" (p. 224).

12. In the area of the lie that transgenderism is normal, what are some specific ways Christians can respond in faith, obedience, and good works?

_____

_____

_____

_____

"We were born male or female, and we will be male and female in either heaven or hell. People with intersex condition are no more excluded from this glorious promise than anyone with a medical illness, as the dominant sexual presentation for each person with an intersex condition will be healed and glorified in the new Jerusalem if that person trusts in Christ for salvation. Additionally, the ontology of biological sex is very good news for Christian people who suffer from gender dysphoria, because in heaven and then in the new Jerusalem, God will restore and perfect all of us, giving us glorified bodies that hold no sin or corruption. What a promise! This is true whether you have had a sex-change operation or not. God cares very little for our foolish attempts to rewrite his law. His goodness far outweighs our foolishness" (p. 226).

13. How might the promise of resurrection help someone who struggles with transgenderism?

_____

_____

_____

_____

14. Read Matthew 22:37–38 and Romans 12:1. How can these verses help you puzzle through the lies about transgenderism?

_____

_____

_____

_____

"The biblical witness is clear. We are to conform our mind to Christ and discipline the body to desire only that which God has for us. Because we all are born with the desire for something that God hates, we should not see transgenderism as foreign but as a sin. We want to show great compassion for those who are trapped in the lie of transgenderism, but we don't accomplish this by reframing sin as a grace" (p. 231).

15. In what areas do you struggle to discipline your mind?

_____

_____

16. What resources or habits do you engage to help you in this area?

Eternal Life Means More than Just Living Forever

"A godly perspective of the reality of heaven and hell is crucial in fighting the sins of the flesh" (p. 233).

1. What has been your view of hell?

_____

_____

_____

_____

_____

2. What evidence from chapter 12 do you find a compelling argument for the eternality of hell, that "those in hell suffer for eternity in a state of consciousness"?

_____

_____

_____

3. Read 2 Thessalonians 1:9 and Revelation 14:11; 20:10. What do these verses say about hell?

4. What do you still have questions about or want to study further on the topic of hell?

5. Aside from the specific duration of hell, the very idea of hell is disbelieved by some professing Christians. What changes in a person's faith if they don't believe in hell? What difference might this make in a person's battle against the sins of the flesh?

6. How does an understanding of the reality of heaven help us fight the sins of the flesh?

_____

_____

_____

_____

"Denying the eternality of hell violates the command to love God and our neighbor. It bears repeating that cheapening God's holy commands so that we don't hurt someone's feelings is not loving" (p. 238).

7. How can we engage with our neighbors about the idea of hell in a way that is helpful for their souls?

_____

_____

_____

_____

Is Gender Dysphoria Illness and Transgenderism Social Contagion?

"This is how a social contagion works: the patient presents a series of symptoms, and the therapist offers one solution. But the symptoms that women bring to the table are common to us all: feeling uncomfortable and unsafe in our bodies and hating the way our hormones change our moods. These symptoms are reflective of several things—including normal adolescence" (p. 242).

8. In what ways can you identify with the emotions and experiences that might lead someone to become transgender?

_____

_____

_____

9. How have you dealt with those feelings and experiences in a way that brought wholeness under the lordship of Christ?

10. How might your own struggles and experiences help someone who is struggling with transgenderism? What could you share that might help them, and how would you share it?

11. What things should Christians avoid doing—what would be unhelpful to someone struggling with transgenderism?

"Jesus is the hero of this story, and Jim is his ambassador. Rough around the edges and colorful with his adjectives, Jim loved Jesus. Because Jim was closer to Jesus than to Art, and also because Jim had a past friendship with Art, Jim was able to be of real use. Both Jim's history and his faith played a role. He wasn't in any way persuaded to 'stand in Art's shoes' (and not only because Art was wearing high heels). Jim was filled with godly sympathy, and he had no desire to lead Art by empathy into worldly sorrow" (p. 246).

12. What principles can you draw from the story of Jim and Art that you can apply to your interactions with transgendered people or your church's treatment of them?

13. Are you currently praying for people who are struggling with gender confusion? How could you engage in a ministry of prayer for them? What would you pray for, and why is it important?

Repenting from Transgenderism

"Everyone has a path to sin. Perhaps your path to sin is responsive to the sin of others. This is often the case with childhood sexual abuse or trauma. Perhaps you are sinning because of a deep desire that wells up inside you, something that is as much yours as your face or name. This is likely original sin, the way that Adam's sin now fingerprints your life. It does not matter what the sin is. It does not matter if you are sinning as a response to being sinned against, as the result of some indwelling pattern of desire that comes from the fall, or because of some willful impulse over which you failed to exercise prayer and self-control. We all sin. And Christians are all called to repent. True repentance involves a change of mind, a change of affections, and a change in your life" (p. 248).

14. How big a role does repentance play in your life? Do you think it should be a bigger part of your spiritual walk? If so, how could you make that change?

15. Read Psalm 51. What are the characteristics of true repentance? Are all of these present in your typical prayers of confession?

Vice or Virtue

16. On a scale of 1 to 10, with 10 being "very content," how content are you with your life circumstances? With your gender?

17. Read Philippians 4:4–13. What are some of Paul's secrets to being content?

_____

_____

_____

18. Which of the following practices of contentment outlined by Jeremiah Burroughs come easily to you? Which are more of a challenge? (Refer to the book as needed for clarification of each one.)

- Be unsatisfied with the world.
- Subtract desires, don't add them.
- Add burdens, don't seek to subtract them.
- Look at your afflictions through the mind of Christ and the cross of Christ.
- Do your duties before God and men—do the good works to which God has set you apart.
- Conform or "melt" your will to God's.

_____

_____

_____

_____

19. Think of the things about which you find it hardest to be content. What spiritual practices do you need to employ to work on that area?

_____

_____

"Christian contentment is an active and rigorous application of faith; it is not passive resignation. Christian contentment is the biblical antidote to the sin of envy. Understanding contentment as a spiritual weapon with power to defeat the sin of envy helps the Christian who struggles with gender identity to rely upon her union with Christ to grow her in his likeness. The point is to look like God's will for you, not the will of your flesh" (p. 255).

20. How can understanding and practicing contentment help those struggling with gender confusion?

MODESTY IS AN OUTDATED BURDEN THAT SERVES MALE DOMINANCE AND HOLDS WOMEN BACK

CHAPTER 13

In the Presence of My Enemies

1. Have you ever experienced Christian community like the one Rosaria describes? What do you think are the hallmarks of Christian fellowship—what sets it apart from other gatherings?

_____

_____

_____

_____

"Even though victimhood served as my catechism, I just couldn't talk myself into believing this while we were singing Psalm 23. God's word started to rewrite my words. And that is when I looked into the mirror of God's word and saw it: I, the English professor, was misreading the text. I wasn't dining in the presence of my enemies. I was the enemy. It was dreadful to behold—I was God's enemy" (p. 261).

2. Have you ever had an experience that made you realize something new and surprising about yourself, like the one the author describes? Describe the circumstances that led to the realization and what you learned.

_____

_____

"These women were strong and valued and loved. They cared for their children and husbands well. They were covered by godly men, and they lived as a team with a divine purpose and eternal calling. They were honored. But they didn't sell themselves. They didn't talk about themselves. They possessed a virtue that I had not ever seen before: modesty" (pp. 263–64).

3. What do you think of when you hear the word *modesty*? What habits and heart attitudes characterize this virtue?

_____

_____

_____

_____

4. What things are sometimes viewed as synonymous with modesty that are not the same as a true biblical definition of modesty? (They may be part of it or related to it, but they are not the whole of it.)

_____

_____

_____

_____

5. What is the relationship between modesty and biblical patriarchy?

_____

_____

6. How can someone grow in modesty? What is involved in cultivating this virtue?

CHAPTER 14

Exhibitionism

The New Almost-Christian Virtue

"The lie that modesty for Christian women is an outdated cultural expectation has shipwrecked many Christian women and leaves the generation of our daughters in peril. In both dress and social media use, modesty has been replaced by exhibitionism" (p. 268).

1. How would you define *exhibitionism*? Where do you see this vice in the church?

Modesty and Temptation

"In *Modesty: More than a Change of Clothes*, Martha Peace and Kent Keller define modesty as 'an inner attitude of the heart motivated by a love for God that seeks His glory through purity and humility; it often reveals itself in words, actions, expressions, and clothes.' . . . Martha contrasts biblical modesty with immodesty, which she defines as 'an attitude of the heart that expresses itself with inappropriate words, actions, expressions and/or clothes that are flirtatious, manipulative, revealing, or suggestive of sensuality or pride.' Immodesty is a sin that can be diagnosed easily (unlike other sins that lurk underground). We wear immodesty on our body and blogs. Perhaps only the proudly immodest are deluded" (pp. 269–70 and 270n2, n4).

2. Looking at these definitions of modesty and immodesty, what are some specific words or actions that would show someone to be

- Modest
- Immodest

_____

_____

_____

_____

3. How can the church encourage modesty without "blaming the victim"?

_____

_____

_____

_____

_____

Men and Women Are Not Interchangeable

4. Read Titus 2:1–8. What do these verses teach us about the virtue of modesty and how we can grow in it?

_____

_____

_____

_____

_____

5. What areas do you sense the Holy Spirit convicting you about regarding modesty and exhibitionism? What action steps will you take in response to the things you've been reading and thinking about in this chapter?

_____

_____

_____

_____

The Danger of Temptation

"Temptation comes from the hand of Satan himself, employing three potential means: his own power and knowledge of our weakness, the world's goods and glitter, and our own sin nature and the personal history we have with sin. Although we live in a world that eschews modesty and believes that everyone needs to know all of our struggles, we see that this is unsafe. As you are 'coming out' and 'giving voice to your pain,' Satan is listening. He is taking notes, and perhaps because of your need for self-disclosure done in the name of authenticity, he now knows how to bait the hook" (p. 276).

6. Thinking of the temptations you struggle with, how have you seen these three means of temptation at work?

_____

_____

_____

_____

7. How might exhibitionism create the occasion for temptation? How have you seen this at work in real life?

_____

_____

"Owen is not saying that a temptation is a personality pattern. Owen would cringe at someone saying something like, 'Homosexual desire is my temptation pattern, not my sin.' He would cringe because of the false teaching that drives that unbiblical statement right into the clutches of Satan. Indeed, for Owen (and Scripture), once temptation becomes a pattern, it lodges not in your Myers-Briggs or Enneagram score but rather in your soul. A temptation pattern is what we call 'indwelling sin,' and it will kill you if you don't kill it" (p. 276 and 276n11).

8. In your daily life, do you think or speak of temptation as being this serious? What would change if you did?

9. What would you need to change in order to deal with temptation as seriously as Owen encourages us to?

10. Read James 1:12–15. What principles do these verses teach about temptation, and how might you apply these principles to your life?

11. What sins are commonly reframed as temptation in modern culture?

12. What are the consequences of such reframing in the church? In culture at large?

13. How can you tell if you are experiencing an outward temptation or an inward sin? Where is the line, and how can you train your conscience to be more alert to it?

14. How does modesty relate to temptation?

Modesty, Temptation, Sexual Abuse, and Cults

15. Given the abuses in the church that have led to modesty being maligned, misunderstood, and misused, how should the church walk the line between encouraging the biblical virtue of modesty and allowing it to be used as an occasion for abuse?

16. How can the church respond to abusers and abused in a way that places responsibility for sin on the sinner and also holds women to the standards of godly womanhood?

Modesty and Social Media

"Perhaps no other medium has created a cult of immodesty as much as social media. Here, we garner 'likes,' sympathy, and solidarity, hunker down in divisive camps, create a following, stir up strife and pride, create new sins and redefine old ones, and engage in slander and prideful derision all in the name of discernment and telling the truth, and we waste an enormous amount of time that would be better spent in doing almost anything else. (And I mean *anything* else: alphabetizing your spice rack comes to mind)" (p. 281).

17. What does modesty look like on social media?

_____

_____

_____

_____

18. What are the greatest temptations of social media? What specific sins does it encourage you to commit?

_____

_____

_____

_____

19. What are good uses of social media, and how do you safeguard yourself so you can use it for good while avoiding its temptations?

_____

_____

_____

_____

"The bottom line is this: when modesty is exchanged for exhibitionism and then promoted as a new Christian virtue, especially in our social media–infused world, no one is more hurt by it than women. For women who wish to conduct themselves with modesty, as the Lord desires, we need to be mindful of our social-media footprint. Regardless of what others do or say, we are called to be above reproach. The Internet escalates gossip, slander, and irreconcilable breaches of fellowship" (p. 286).

20. How does social media tempt and hurt women in particular?

_____

_____

_____

_____

21. What is one specific way you will intentionally connect with someone in person rather than online this week?

_____

_____

_____

_____

Afterword

The Difference between Acceptance and Approval, or,
How to Stay Connected to Loved Ones Who Believe
These Lies without Falling for Them Yourself

THESE ARE THE LIES we've looked at in this book:

   Lie #1: Homosexuality is normal.

   Lie #2: Being a spiritual person is kinder than being a biblical Christian.

   Lie #3: Feminism is good for the world and the church.

   Lie #4: Transgenderism is normal.

   Lie #5: Modesty is an outdated burden that serves male dominance and holds
        women back.

1. Which one of these did you find most enlightening or surprising?

_____

_____

_____

_____

_____

2. Which one convicted or challenged you the most? What action steps have you taken or do you plan to take in response?

_____

_____

_____

_____

3. Is there any one of these lies that you or a loved one are struggling through—something that you aren't sure if you believe to be a lie? Describe that struggle honestly, and then pray that God will reveal the truth to you.

_____

_____

_____

_____

4. Which one or two are most prevalent in your church, and what do you intend to do to raise awareness or challenge people about it?

_____

_____

_____

_____

5. What group or person have you gained fresh compassion for as a result of reading this book? How will you reach out to them?

_____

_____

6. Rosaria describes two churches, only one of which serves as a watchman, on pages 291–292. Which of these better describes your church, and why?

"Acceptance is a mature response. It means living life with your eyes open and facing reality. Acceptance requires the ability to be compassionate and sympathetic. Approval is an immature response. It means allowing empathy to overrule what you know to be true in the hopes that 'standing in the shoes' of your loved one will help" (p. 293).

7. In practical terms, what is the difference between acceptance and approval? How can we accept people whose sinful lifestyle we cannot approve?

8. What are some hard realities that you have to accept about your life or your loved ones, and what are some false interpretations or lies that you need to reject?

9. Second Corinthians 1:4 tells us to "comfort those who are in any affliction, with the comfort with which we ourselves are comforted." What is one struggle you have had that you can use to help others?

"You can affirm that you are a Christian, but if you do not obey God's requirements as revealed in the Bible, then you are proving your affirmation false. Obedience does not make you a legalist or a fundamentalist. Obedience to the word of God reveals that you are a Christian. We can only help our lost loved ones if we ourselves stay tethered to God's word by grace" (p. 296).

10. If you love a prodigal, review the principles offered on pages 297–300 for how to love her well. Which of these do you need to put into practice, and how will you do so?

11. Reread your answers to the Five Lies section on pages 12–13. Which of your beliefs have been strengthened and informed since you began this study? Which have changed?

"The Lord Jesus Christ and his grace that weaves this life together is strong enough to hold you fast, in grief and joy, as you serve in the body of Christ, the church militant, until the Lord returns and we become the church triumphant. We leave our grief and tears here, for there are no tears where we are going. Christian, this is our moment. We must speak boldly to our world. We need to live boldly for Christ. We need to do this now. Heaven has no regrets, and neither do Christians" (pp. 312–13).